The Promise within the Garden

A Meditative Journey into the Heart of God

By Dr. Kim Grom

*The Promise within the Garden: A Meditative Journey into the He*art of God

Copyright © 2020 by Dr. Kim Grom

Scripture quotations marked NIV are taken from THE HOLY BIBLE, NEW INTERNATIONAL VERSION®, NIV® Copyright © 1973, 1978, 1984, 2011 by Biblica, Inc.® Used by permission. All rights reserved worldwide.

Scripture quotations marked KJV are taken from the King James Version of the Bible. Public domain in the USA.

Scripture quotations marked MSG are taken from THE MESSAGE, copyright © 1993, 2002, 2018 by Eugene H. Peterson. Used by permission of NavPress. All rights reserved. Represented by Tyndale House Publishers, Inc.

Scripture quotations marked NKJV are taken from the New King James Version®. Copyright © 1982 by Thomas Nelson. Used by permission. All rights reserved.

Scripture quotations marked NLT are taken from the Holy Bible, New Living Translation, copyright © 1996, 2004, 2015 by Tyndale House Foundation. Used by permission of Tyndale House Publishers, Inc., Carol Stream, Illinois 60188. All rights reserved.

ISBN: 978-1-7344895-0-7 (Print)
      978-1-7344895-1-4 (Digital)

Printed in the USA.

This little book is dedicated to my grandmother Helen, who lovingly tended to her rose garden. I learned many things as a young child as I watched her care for her stunning collection of roses.

To my daughter, Kate, who recently discovered the world of gardening: may the delight, the mystery, and the beauty of gardening be your pleasure for a lifetime.

Sometimes in spring, it's just plain old gray, gray, gray outside. The early months of the year blend into another and the cold doesn't quit. Mild boredom and depression often seep in. Just when you think you won't ever pack up that winter coat and the landscape is looking bleak, consider planting a garden!

Robert John Thornton, *New illustration of the sexual system of Carolus von Linnaeus* (London, 1807), Plate XL, The Snowdrop, http://biodiversitylibrary.org/page/306928.

Even if you are not "Mary Mary" it's important to know how your garden grows. It is as natural for greenery to happen on the earth as it is for you or me to take a breath. For with a garden, the earth simply boasts: "Sit and watch while I generate something magnificent!"

George S. Elgood and Gertrude Jekyll, *Some English Gardens*, (London, 1904), Plate 41, St. Annes, Clontarf, https://biodiversitylibrary.org/page/18503450.

You, of course, must provide the elbow grease, the plants, and the water, but hostess Earth does the rest!" Simply begin with the dirt as your canvas, add your favorite garden plants, and you are on your way to creating a spectacular, living scene. A garden of any sort without the hostess, our Earth, is simply impossible!

George S. Elgood and Gertrude Jekyll, *Some English Gardens*, (London, 1904), Plate 4, *Blyborough: Hollyhocks*, http://biodiversitylibrary.org/page/18503187.

A garden reminds us that everything in life emerges according to season, perfectly timed and orchestrated. Under the warm sun there suddenly appears a kaleidoscope. of colors. Spring daffodils are followed by iris, peonies, and assorted tulips. Daylilies emerge and linger all summer along with the prima donna of the garden, the fabulous rose. Spring and summer are made complete with the heady scent of fragrant purple lavender. [When harvested, lavender makes a splendid potpourri.] As days grow chilly in October, we look forward to fall mums, bejeweled in colorful splendor.

George S. Elgood and Gertrude Jekyll, *Some English Gardens*, (London, 1904), Plate 25, Ramscliffe: Larkspur, http://biodiversitylibrary.org/page/ 18503344.

Everyone has a favorite flower, tree, or shrub that captures the attention and the eye. Of course, they often catch the nose as well—sometimes for better or worse! Tissues and birdwatching are part of many a gardening adventure!

A typical spring array of flowering shrubs and trees may include purple and pink hydrangeas, soft white and violet lilacs, pastel azaleas, pretty pink and white flowering dogwoods, and beautiful red crabapple trees. These lovely specimens showcase their unique and colorful blooms just like the ladies of days gone by wearing fancy spring frocks.

George S. Elgood and Gertrude Jekyll, *Some English Gardens*, (London, 1904), Plate 23, *Montacute: Sunflowers*, http://biodiversitylibrary.org/page/18503332.

This past Easter/Passover season, I had the pleasure of seeing my flower garden, which was planted two seasons ago, burst into life. The year prior I had the joy of seeing all of the new plants bloom in perfect procession, each one according to their unique timing in the season.

George S. Elgood and Gertrude Jekyll, *Some English Gardens*, (London, 1904), Plate 38, *The Deanery Garden, Rochester*, http://biodiversitylibrary.org/page/18503430.

This year, I observe my garden plants have taken a firmer hold of the earth and their flowers confidently burst forth. Leafy greenery is thick, fresh, and clean, and so the garden has "taken." Moss has not yet found its way into the crevices, but I expect that to happen over time. Moss is the telltale sign of a mature garden.

George S. Elgood and Gertrude Jekyll, *Some English Gardens*, (London, 1904), Plate 21, *Kellie Castle*, http://biodiversitylibrary.org/page/18503316.

What secrets will this newly-created beauty, my flower garden, one day hold?

Perhaps the memory of footsteps of one who came to sit and admire her? One who paused to sit and rest and contemplate, surrounded by her earthiness and sweet fragrances. On a stormy day, with flowers dancing and swaying in the wind, possibly a few visitors in raingear were peeking about. Then bowing under heavy sheets of rain, with plants tightly hugging the ground, maybe an observer from the window gets to witness them suddenly springing up toward heaven! The sun reappears, and the garden has recovered.

George S. Elgood, George S. Elgood and Gertrude Jekyll, *Some English Gardens*, (London, 1904), Plate 24, *Ramscliffe: Orange Lilies and Monkshood*, http://biodiversitylibrary.org/page/18503338.

Gardens can have many secrets. Imagine lovers who shared a kiss in a private, quiet spot between the lilies. As fragile and fleeting as blossoms, the sweetness of such moments pass in a twinkling of an eye. A garden is surely one of a photographer's favorite backdrops. When you consider the inner workings of a garden, you discover that many of life's secrets and wisdom are hidden within.

George S. Elgood and Gertrude Jekyll, *Some English Gardens*, (London, 1904), Plate 44, *Phlox and Daisy*, http://biodiversitylibrary.org/page/18503472.

MEDITATIONS

Waiting

We hold our ground for a season, like a flower waiting to bloom.

Galatians 6:9 [NIV] tells us to "not become weary in well doing, for at the proper time we will reap a harvest if we do not give up."

George S. Elgood and Gertrude Jekyll, *Some English Gardens*, (London, 1904), Plate 33, *Viscountess Folkstone*, http://biodiversitylibrary.org/page/18503396.

Resting

Another takes her turn, and while she shines and blooms, you must wait. Rest in the understanding that all things in life have a season.

Ecclesiastes [NIV] says, "To everything there is a season and a time to every purpose under heaven."

George S. Elgood and Gertrude Jekyll, *Some English Gardens*, (London, 1904), Plate 11, *The Lower Terrace, Berkeley Castle*, http://biodiversitylibrary.org/page/18503252.

Rooted

During times of hardship, it's best to firmly root—and avoid being tossed to and fro. Emerge stronger and more exquisite in the next season!

Isaiah 41:10 (NIV) says , "Do not fear, for I am with you; do not be dismayed, for I am your God. I will strengthen you and help you; I will uphold you with my righteous right hand."

George S. Elgood and Gertrude Jekyll, *Some English Gardens*, (London, 1904), Plate 1, *Phlox*, http://biodiversitylibrary.org/page/18503212.

Beauty

Discover, like the garden flower, that you have your own unique and special beauty.

Song of Solomon 4:1 (NLT) says, "You are beautiful, my darling, beautiful beyond words. Your eyes are like doves behind your veil."

George S. Elgood and Gertrude Jekyll, *Some English Gardens*, (London, 1904), Plate 40, *China Roses and Lavender, Palmerstown*, http://biodiversitylibrary.org/page/18503441.

Retreat

When life is cold, wintery, and foreboding, retreat under a safe covering of snow. Find rest on the garden bench when summer comes around again.

Psalm 119:114 (MSG) says, "You're my place of quiet retreat, I wait for your Word to renew me."

George S. Elgood and Gertrude Jekyll, *Some English Gardens*, (London, 1904), Plate 7, *Bulwick: The Gateway*, http://biodiversitylibrary.org/page/18503224.

Patience

Learn patience during tough seasons, during times of wind and rain. Hold your ground.

Psalms 27:13-14 (NIV) says, "I remain confident of this: I will see the goodness of
the Lord in the land of the living. Wait for the Lord; be strong and take heart and
wait for the Lord."

George S. Elgood and Gertrude Jekyll, *Some English Gardens*, (London, 1904), Plate 50, *Lady Coventry's Needlework*, http://biodiversitylibrary.org/page/18503511.

Faith

Trust in God by faith for the next situation, believe that the sun will shine again.

Isaiah 26:3 (KJV) says, "You will keep him in perfect peace whose mind is stayed on you, because he trusts in you."

George S. Elgood and Gertrude Jekyll, *Some English Gardens*, (London, 1904), Plate 46, *Abbey-Leix*, http://biodiversitylibrary.org/page/18503486.

Trust

Hold firmly onto hope that you will bloom again in the next season.

Psalm 62:8 (KJV) says, "Trust in him at all times...pour out your heart before him; our God is a refuge for us."

George S. Elgood and Gertrude Jekyll, *Some English Gardens*, (London, 1904), Plate 19, *Crathes*, http://biodiversitylibrary.org/page/18503304.

Thankful

As blooms finally come forth, if they are not quite as lush, be ever thankful for the Master's pruning.

John 15:2 (NKJV) says, "Every branch that bears fruit He prunes, that it may bear more fruit."

George S. Elgood and Gertrude Jekyll, *Some English Gardens*, (London, 1904), Plate 47, *Michaelmas Daisies, Munstead Wood*, http://biodiversitylibrary.org/page/18503494.

Timeless

In 1913, inspired by Lord R. Gower's exquisite English garden, the poet D F Gurney penned this famous poem:

The kiss of the sun for pardon
the song of the birds for mirth
one is nearer God's heart in a garden
than anywhere else on earth.

George S. Elgood and Gertrude Jekyll, *Some English Gardens*, (London, 1904), Plate 17, *The Apollo, Balcaskie*, http://biodiversitylibrary.org/page/18503292.

So many sentiments are revealed as one meditates upon the garden! Our toil affords us the opportunity to partner with the earth, wind, sun, and sky. With a garden we have the delightful anticipation of the return of its beauty year after year.

George S. Elgood and Gertrude Jekyll, *Some English Gardens*, (London, 1904), Plate 10, *Melbourne: Amorini*, http://biodiversitylibrary.org/page/18503244.

What will you plant this season? Annuals or perennials with bright yellows, whites, and purple Easter lilacs?

Are you adventurous and perhaps you have some land? If so, then you may decide to plant flowering trees such as lilacs, dogwoods, or forsythias.

Or you might bravely attempt a delicate rose garden, complete with tea roses, climbers, and luscious blooms worthy of the glass vase on the table?

The Dingee and Conrad Company, *Our New Guide to Rose Culture*, (West Grove, PA, 1894), page 4, http://biodiversitylibrary.org/page/43902957.

Are herbs and culinary treats your passion? Try vegetables! Nothing compares to the taste of homegrown oregano and basil. Just the right touch for a summer meal.

Paul A. Robert, Les papillons dans la nature (Paris, 1934) , Plate 6, Le Soufré, https://www. biodiversitylibrary.org/page/33079887.

With attention to detail plus proper tending, I promise your world will be a more beautiful place for having put your hands to the dirt. You are about to experience something very special, even if you simply remain a window observer. Let the beauty of the garden captivate you!

George S. Elgood and Gertrude Jekyll, *Some English Gardens*, (London, 1904), Plate 26, *Levens*, http://biodiversitylibrary.org/page/18503349.

When properly cared for, the garden will produce its best for you, season after season. A garden, after all, contains secrets, wisdom, and the faithful promise of a beautiful tomorrow.

George S. Elgood and Gertrude Jekyll, *Some English Gardens*, (London, 1904), Plate 5, The Pergola, Great Tangley, http://biodiversitylibrary.org/page/18503193.

About the Author

An avid gardener, Dr. Kim Grom especially loves English style gardening. She resides on a farm in New Jersey, complete with lovely gardens. Scriptural meditations are one of her favorite pastimes. Kim can be reached at kgrom@grom.com.

www.ingramcontent.com/pod-product-compliance
Lightning Source LLC
Chambersburg PA
CBHW080633030426
42336CB00018B/3176